# ECHOES FROM SWANSEA
MASIMBA MUKICHI

The rights of Masimba Mukichi has been asserted by him in accordance with the Copyright, Designs and Patents Act 1988

All rights reserved. No part of this publication may be reproduced, stored in a retrieval system or transmitted in any form or by any means, electronic, mechanical, photocopying, and recording or others, without the prior permission of Masimba Mukichi or a license permitting restricted copying. In the UK such licenses are issued by the Licensing Agency, Saffron House, 6 -10 Kirby Street, London, EC1N 8TS

**Table of Contents**

**1 The Shakespearean sonnet:** Lovey
**2 The Shakespearean sonnet**: Leap into My Arms
**3 The Shakespearean sonnet:** Heartbroken
**4 Petrarchan sonnet:** Irresponsible Daddy
**5Petrarchan sonnet:** Couch Potato
**6 Spenserian sonnet:** Alone in the Jungle
**7The Terza rima:** Devil Incarnate
**8 The Terza rima:** The Journey
**9The Villanelle:** He is gone
**10The Villanelle:** Month end Blues
**11The Terzanelle:** Ebola is Deadly
**12The Terzanelle**: Diamonds Goons
**13 The Ballad:** Around a Night-fire
**14The Ballad**: Gone to Soon
**15 The Ballade:** United we Stand
**16 The Ballade Royal:** You Nailed It
**17The Pindaric ode**: Awake My Son
**18 The Homostrophic ode**: Swansea City FC
**19 Blank verse:** Close to Nature
**20 The Renga:** Write on Poet
**21 The Tanka:** Give them a chance
**22 Narrative poem**: Boxing Day Tsunami
**23 Narrative poem:** Murder in the Neighbourhood
**24 Free verse**: Free spirit- it's Halloween
**25 Free verse:** Single and Ready to Mingle
**26 Free verse**: Part of me is missing
**27 Free verse:** Swansea on a Saturday Night
**28 Free verse:** Christmas Day in Swansea
**29 Free verse:** Payday Lender
**30 Free verse:** Drug Addict
**31 Free verse:** Goodbye winter Floods

**32 Free verse:** Halt this Football Madness

**33 Free verse:** Benefits Cheat

**34 Free verse:** Wonder with me

**35 Free verse:** At the Beach after Dark

**36 Free verse:** The Sea

**37 Free verse:** Adulterous Cleric

**38 Free verse:** Traffic Jam

**39 Free verse:** Leap into the Dark

**40 Free verse:** If I Could turn back the clock

**41 Free verse:** Sanctity of life

**42 Free verse:** Money Can't Buy Hygiene

**43 Free verse:** Hear Me Cry

**44 Free verse:** St Jude- mother of all storms

**45 Free verse:** Roaring Lioness

**46 Free verse:** Reclusive Neighbour

**47 Free verse:** The Stick Fighter from Qunu

**48 Free verse:** Family Squabble

**49 Free verse:** I've got my eyes to thank

**50 Free verse:** I can hear

**51 Free verse:** The Taste of the Pudding…

**52 Free verse:** Letter from the war front

**53 Free verse:** Dead without a trace

**54 Free verse:** The Great Escape

**55 Free verse:** Dawn of a new era

**56 Free verse:** Don't you dare…

**57 Free verse:** Guess what!

**58 Free verse:** You Gave me wings to fly

**59 Free verse:** Human Kindness

**60 An Elegy:** Leaf Taken

**61 Monologue:** Only Dreaming

**62 Monologue:** I misfired

**1 The Shakespearean sonnet**
**Title: Lovey**

Now that we are in love sweetheart,
Accept this rose – darling Rosy.
I promise to love you with all my heart.
Our love is like the rising sun – its cosy.
It's warm and promising to be very hot.
From now on, dwell in my heart.
Blossom in my heart till we tie the knot,
Shine on and shine on sweetheart.

May morrow bring forth springtime.
So that we may smell the fresh scent of the Daffodil,
May morrow bring forth summertime.
So that we may dance in the sunny weather in tranquil.
We're now two peas in a pod sweetie.
 Into your heart I commend my love pretty.

## 2 The Shakespearean sonnet
## Title: Leap into My Arms

Take my hand – my love is free.
Spread your roots into my heart.
Walk with me into the future – agree.
Our love weathers the storm, it dies hard.
Leap into my arms like the wind stunning blond.
The tide of love is rising – it's unstoppable.
Kiss my kissable lips without fear – let's bond.
Our love is as solid as a rock, it's unbreakable.
It shimmers with life like a Flame Lily flower,
It blooms and blossoms but not wither.
My voice of reason is clearer and louder.
I love you – I really do! My Flame Lily flower!
Run, run, the door to my heart is open, love.
Leap into my arms gently, I'm as meek as a dove.

## 3 The Shakespearean sonnet
### Title: Heartbroken

The sky is dimly lit.

Dimly lit with the pale and sultry moon,

Yes, it's true we have split.

I'm here to lament - he is gone too soon.

He went for a night out after being paid.

And he decided to go astray,

To go astray with a barmaid,

What's left for me is to pray.

To pray for his safe return home.

He is gone like a bug.

For sure he is gone.

When I need a hug,

Gone with a slut! I'm heartbroken!

Absolutely, I'm forsaken!

**4 Petrarchan sonnet**

**Title: Irresponsible Daddy**

He is behaving like a buffoon.
He is neglecting his family like a fool.
He is smitten by lap dancers as if it's cool.
It's a matter of time, he'll regret it soon.
He thinks he is a tycoon.
He is feckless, lap dancers make him drool.
His morals stink like human stool.
His kids fear him like a typhoon.

May he stop wallowing in self-pity?
He can change for the better.
He can be a good daddy with practice.
He can do better - by not being a slut-getter?
He can face the future with hope, it's not tricky.
Drooling for hookers - lap dancers is malpractice.

**5 Petrarchan sonnet**

**Title: Couch Potato**

Round the clock, you're on that couch.
That couch is your command centre.
You give orders from that settee like an actor.
IPhone 4 is always in your pouch.
Slowly but surely, you devour junk food.
Pal, watch your weight better!
You're becoming obese – it's not good.
'Own up' take charge of your health Mister!
You can conquer your demons.

Walk the dog – get a job mate.
Eat healthily – go to the gym with pride.
Don't be lazy - take a decisive stride.
Before your weight embarrasses your child at the school gate,
Get a life couch potato – obesity is sour like lemons.

**6 Spenserian sonnet**

**Title: Alone in the Jungle**

Watching the setting sun,

Alone in the jungle,

As an only son,

With dosh in a bundle,

I'm ready to mingle.

To mingle and mingle with wild life,

In the thickest jungle,

The laughter of the hyenas is full of life.

It's reminding me of the partying life.

Blonde, the baboon's singing for supper is scary.

'Hom, hom'– I don't need a knife!

I need food, I eat curry!

Twilight brings screams of ghosts closer and closer.

I run and run for dear life like a bike racer.

**7 The Terza rima**
**Title: Devil Incarnate**

At that children's home daily he walks tall.
It's true all kids keep him in high esteem.
He is a father figure to them all.

They all want to work with him as a team.
They always run to him for protection.
They endure pain without a scream.

He is their carer – they pay attention!
They share with him their guarded secrets.
They take all what he says without objection.

They're as pure as the plumes of the egrets.
No one knows what lurks in the shadow of his mind.
He is a paedophile – he abuses them in secret.

He is a predator, a threat to humankind.
A wolf in sheep's robes – he hides behind the veil.
He is evil – a disgrace to mankind!

Dirty paedophile, oh hear! You're evil.
Devil incarnate – you're 'sinful weevil'.

**8 Terza rima**
**Title: The Journey**

So this is what it's like being pregnant.
To feel the baby kick in my tummy,
It's real a blessed heartfelt attachment.

Oh gosh – it makes me a yummy mummy.
It gives me a smile, cool as a sea breeze.
Pregnancy thrills – can't wait to be mammy.

Morning sickness makes my whole body freeze.
Minted sweets and hot chocolate helps me cope.
No more dope and all the binge drinking sprees,

Seeing my tummy grow big gives me hope.
Cravings bother me – yoga keeps me fit.
I bow down in prayer – shall I call him Pope?

Being nine months pregnant makes me sit!
Can't cook for spouse – so as to win his heart,
Water birth is for me – I admit.

Motherhood is a sweet journey to start!
Oh hear! It's a journey close to my heart!

**9 The Villanelle**
**Title: He is Gone**

Oh gosh! He is gone tonight.
Gone away along the motorway,
He is now out of sight.

Is it a matter of fight or flight?
He has spoiled my day.
Oh gosh! He is gone tonight.

He wasn't ready for a fight.
He has decided to go astray.
He is now out of sight.

Did I ignite?
When I called him gay,
Oh gosh! He is gone tonight.

Wish I had hold him tight,
My day wouldn't have turned grey.
He is now out of sight.

He was my glowing light.
I regret to have called him gay.
Oh gosh! He is gone tonight.
He is now out of sight.

## 10 The Villanelle
## Month end Blues

I'm not only broke but broken.
Month end blues – dosh is scanty!
I'm penniless and forsaken.

May well- wishers give me a token?
Need a rowdy night – can't organise a house party.
I'm not only broke but broken.

Don't call me drunken – I'm Duncan.
The landlady needs her rent – I feel guilty.
I'm penniless and forsaken.

Creditor talks to me shaken with eyes sunken.
She demands dosh but I don't have – I'm not being naughty.
I'm not only broke but broken.

My borrowing power was taken.
Can't pay them a penny – no-one feels pity.
I'm penniless and forsaken.

I must awake – they call me rotten.
For failing to pay a fiver for the bacon – it's nasty!
I'm not only broke but broken.
I'm penniless and forsaken!

## 11 The Terzanelle
### Ebola is Deadly

Ebola is deadly – that's right!
Debora is dead – Flora is dead.
O lord, let's not die and die without a fight.

Ebola is deadly – that's why we dread!
It's do or die – don't dice with death!
Deborah is dead – Flora is dead.

They cared less when they breathed their last breath.
Can't shy away from death – don't die without a fight!
It's do or die – don't dice with death!

Ebola is in sight – finding a cure is our plight.
Ebola is in Liberia – soon it'll be Perth and Neath.
Can't shy away from death – don't die without a fight!

Ebola is in sight – don't let it spread!
At the tunnel's end – there might be light.
Ebola is in Liberia – soon it'll be Perth and Neath.

Death is imminent – it's in sight!
Ebola is deadly – that's right!
At the tunnel's end – there might be light.
O lord, let's not die and die without a fight.

## 12 The Terzanelle
### Diamonds Goons

They're trigger happy – Raymond and Richmond.
They're from the ghetto – they live in the shanty.
They're after diamonds not almonds.

They live on robbery – employment is scanty.
They kill for diamonds – wearing a hood.
They're from the ghetto – they live in the shanty.

They're nasty – they kill whilst they swear.
Blood diamonds! Blood diamonds! They chant!
They kill for diamonds – wearing a hood.

They have blood on their hands – they look sweaty.
They're shabby, evil and deadly.
Blood diamonds! Blood diamonds! They chant!

They're always astounded – they swear.
We can't call them swanky – their guns are always handy.
They're shabby, evil and deadly.

They always think of hanky-panky.
They're trigger happy – Raymond and Richmond.
We can't call them swanky,their guns are always handy.
They're after diamonds not almonds.

## 13 The Ballad
**Title: Tale around a Night-fire**

One murky winter night,
Sitting around a glowing night-fire,
We had no single light.
Then was no solar power to hire.

Grandad was ready to be an orator.
We all had to be attentive.
To be attentive to him as the narrator,
So that morrow we may also be creative,

His story was about hunting.
Hunting in the African jungle,
There was no need to be grunting.
We all had to listen – he didn't giggle!

He killed a lion with a sharpened spear.
It died without a struggle.
Back then – there was no need to fear.
It was all legal – to kill a lion in the jungle.

Grandad was still single.
When he killed the lion,
As the lion dies – its tale wiggle.
He drank its raw blood holding a scion.

That's how he was initiated.
Initiated into manhood,
That's how he was elevated.
Elevated into knighthood,

Masimba Mukichi

As he entered the village walking tall with pride,
They were plenty of beautiful brides to marry.
He was given the honour of choosing a bride,
Bejewelled with bone and lip disc –he was merry!

## 14 The Ballad
### Gone Too Soon

I know not whether it's right.
Or whether it's wrong,
All I know is that she is gone.
In the hallway the smell of death is strong.
No man can comfort me – I cry for the loss.
In grief nights are scary and long.

O lord I know, it's not justified to kill.
In the hallway she lies slain.
They killed her for her beauty.
The smell of death can't be washed by rain.
She is gone but not forgotten.
Forever and ever I shall live with the pain.

Absolutely, I know, time is a healer.
But for now I'm a nerve wreck – I feel the pain.
What goes around comes around.
May the killer also be slain?
He lived by the sword, so may he die of the sword.
She is gone – the hallway has her blood stain.

I know I'm in pain and grief – but I need justice for her.
May her killer hide in shame?
May the killer be forever doomed?
The killer killed her for negative fame.
May the killer rot in hell?
Or May he be ostracised and die lame.

No and no mercy for him – he is ruthless.
Callous murder has no fruitful gain.

Hear me, O lord! I'm speechless.
I'm under strain – can't sustain.
Merciless he is, indeed he is merciless.
She is gone – I can only complain.

Gone, gone to soon – it's too painful.
Gone, gone too soon like fresh air.
Heaven has gained another superb angel.
We were always a pair.
Watch over me lovey – I plead.
In God's glory – no tempers can flare.

The killer is senile. He should be made sterile.
He cut her life short but she lives on, she has nine lives!
Let me walk a mile – towards the Nile.
And scatter her ashes mixed with olives.
So that her ashes float like a lily and rest in style.
Forever and ever in my heart – she thrives!

## 15 The Ballade
## Title: United We Stand...

Hear my pleas brethren of mother earth.
Let not your thoughts aimlessly wonder.
May we pray for peace – peace is dearth.
Let's get focused – let's look yonder!
 Listen and learn – you've to ponder.
Oh please, lend me your ears.
I don't want to be in tears.
Brethren, don't spill blood – that's all.
 Love thy neighbours – share some pears!
United we stand, divided we fall.


Brother men, no wonder why I wonder.
Our world is so full of hate – peace, be still!
We need peace not war – we should not plunder.
Thou shall fear evil – live righteously.
Let's love thy neighbour heartily.
Brother men – he who seeks peace finds peace.
Respect is golden – don't tease.
Learn to say sorry. Watch your steps – let's avert a fall.
Do unto others as you would like them to do unto you – please!
United we stand, divided we fall.


Let's be a society which fears evil.
Let's pray for peace many a night.
Let our hearts not be the bedrock of evil.
The righteous ones are always right.
Good listening skills make us bright.
Respecting others make us winners always.
We shouldn't be unreliable as the railways.

Hope my words are not landing on a hard brick wall.
Arrogance makes friends' part pathways.
United we stand, divided we fall.

Let's not think with our hearts but our heads!
Never wish others dead.
Peace lovers be proud – walk tall.
Show them the way, be exemplary. Look ahead.
United we stand, divided we fall.

**16 The Ballade Royal**
**Response to the ballade United we stand...**
**Title: You Nailed It**

Walk tall, Solomon. You're so clear.
May honour be bestowed unto you – don't breakdown.
You were so explicit – you had no fear.
When you talked about peace – you didn't slow down.
You showed that in spirit you had grown.
I hail you, Solomon. You're so brilliant.
You nailed it. You're proficient – you're resilient.


Yes, we have to love thy neighbour - I agree!
If we speak of the devil for sure he is to appear.
He who seeks peace finds peace – I don't disagree.
You nailed it. We should avoid the spear.
You couldn't have said it any better, love thy neighbours,
share some pears!
Yes, we should be vigilant.
You nailed it. You're proficient – you're resilient.


Do to others as you would like them to do to you –
golden rule forever.
Solomon I hail you –you killed it, you're smarter.
Together as one – it's my pleasure.
We are in this together – you nailed it.
 United we stand, divided we fall - I'm jubilant.
You nailed it. You're proficient – you're resilient.

**17 The Pindaric ode**

**Title: Awake my Son**

Awake, my son, awake.

A man must not sleep all day.

Work and work to keep hunger at bay,

Awake, my son – don't hibernate like a snake.

Don't be a laughing stock.

Time is ticking, watch the clock.

Get a job and get a life.

Sooner or later I shall join the afterlife.

I don't want to leave you without finance.

Sooner or later you shall need romance.

A wife and kids need a cheeseburger.

Oh no, be a good burgher.

Oh 'ducky' – fear the lord.

Oh hear me, my son dearie.

Live within your means – don't make me feel eerie.

Buy what you can afford – drive a Ford!

You've grown into a man – age brings maturity.

Age brings responsibility – age brings purity.

Don't tell me, you're now doing cocaine and ganja.

Don't tell me, you're now a Ninja.

Maintain not being phony.

And I'll buy you a smartphone – Sony.

Awake, my son, awake – once you marry avoid a fling!

Awake, my son, awake – life is for living.

The voice of reasoning is echoing.

The voice of conscience is bellowing.

Awake, my son, awake – life waits for no man.

Live the dream as much as you can.

Oh hear, my son, every dog has got its own day.
Life is good, live the dream.
Every little helps – raindrops eventually flood a stream.
Initiate, the time to act is now – thank God it's Friday!
Dance to the beat.
Feel the heat.
Awake, my son, awake – stand on your feet.
Play hard, work hard – life is sweet.
To love life is to live life.
To live like a king you've to strive.
Awake my son, awake – hard work pays.
Wife and kids need a cheeseburger.
Don't be a mugger – don't die a bugger!

## 18 The Homostrophic Ode
### Title: Swansea City FC

Big up, Swansea City FC – I care!
On that Saturday, October 25, 2014. You made us proud.
I was content to watch you play whilst I breathe the Welsh air.
You trounced Leicester City – 2nil. You pulled the crowd!

Your zeal to play blended like butter and bread.
In your glamorous white football attire – you never tire.
As you played, he was all smiles your coach – in the shade!
You were as hot as the winter fire and always ready to fire.

Indomitable Dragons – may I call you if you don't mind?
In your own backyard, you prevailed – you didn't give the game away.
Indeed, you were in good shape, health mind and kind.
I'm immensely proud; you carried the day – thank you!

I sing and sing praise of you guys – you prevailed with ease.
That's what we call good sportsmanship – perfect recreation!
We were all behind you – it wasn't a tease!
High five, to you our Welsh heroes – you didn't seek fame or attention!

You were like bees on nectar – you were for the game in full force!
Thus let me praise you, for a job well done!
We expected goals, you did impress and enforce.

Keep up the fire! More fire, more wins – your skills are not yet bygone!

**19 Blank verse**

**Title: Close to Nature**

No water so still as that of river Tawe.
If you take a look at it – it's blue and clear.
Marvelling I sit, and watch it flow.
It flows quietly from the Brecon Beacons,
In a South westerly direction it rambles,
It meanders like a python to Swansea.
It's summer – the water is still and clear.
No wonder why it's a hotspot for lovers.
Fresh scent of lilies pulls the crowd.
The air is filled with the noises of birds.
Throat cowing of crows pierces my ears,
The sun's rays reflecting in the river,
Evokes buzzes from wasps and midges,
My mind suppresses the tinkles made,
As I enjoy the sun and the calming breeze,
In the river the frog is at it again.
It's croaking and croaking loudly.
Concurrently other frogs join in.
Some frogs are chirping and grunting.
Others are peeping, whistling and clucking.
Suddenly I'm up on my feet dancing.
Dancing to the melodious sounds of frogs,
A shoal of fish is out and about in the river.
Water splatters into the air at once.
Could it be mermaids or mermen? I wonder.
Assorted buffer fly, flies above my head.
A cool breeze sweeps by, and halts my thoughts.
And I realises it's time to walk home.
Oh dear, it's nice to be close to nature.
Oh hear, enjoy nature while it lasts!

## 20 The Renga
### Title: Write on Poet

Seeing believes, yes.
Upon us is summer sun.
Summer sun is here!

Walk to the woods, warm the feet.
Poet, observe nature write.

Some who walked before?
Left their footprints in the sand,
Time ticks fast without pause.

Walk with a real poet's mind.
Observe nature, write poet.

Listen as owls hoot.
Catch the glimpse of eagles fly.
Feel the breeze enjoy.

Walk with a real poet's mind.
Observe nature pen sonnets.

Summer sun is here!
Smell cool fresh scent of lilies.
Monkeys chatter again.

Relax, rest now. Write on, Write!
In the shade of the Baobab,

**21 The Tanka**
**Title: Give Them a Chance**
But his was true love.
That's why they gladly marry.
Surely they settled.
True love blossomed so quickly.
Gosh! Age is just a number.

Only time knows the truth.
What has tomorrow in store?
Teens love is tricky.
Truth will reign someday perhaps.
Now let's watch the shining stars.

Till dawn brings us light,
What was meant to be shall be.
Lilies bloom and fade.
Let them put their past behind.
True love prevails not age.

They are young in love.
They need the chance and hope.
A long future yes,
Lovers hug, kiss and hold hands.
And think of life together!

## 22 Narrative poem
## Title: Boxing Day Tsunami

On that fateful Sunday morning no one had a clue,
Of what was to happen in our midst,
I was vacationing in Indonesia.
I was out and about on the beach in my bikini.
 Some were paddling and others were kissing.
Out of the blue a giant wave sprang from the sea.
Ferociously the wave charged towards the shore.


There was no time to make a call.
We all started running fearing to fall.
The beach turned into a sea instantly.
Those paddling and those on the beach,
Were all washed into the sea at once.
Boats on the sea didn't survive the wave's might.
The wave created a path of terror in the blink of an eye.


It caused mayhem on everything in sight.
I rushed to safety without pride but with huge strides.
There was nowhere to hide.
I made it to higher ground after a struggle.
Screams, screams of fear caused pandemonium.
Shrieking noises of agony were everywhere.
Beautiful structures were razed to the ground.


The holiday resort became a ghost town at once.
Some survivors held on to pieces of floating wood.
They survived luckily after being thrown on top of a cliff.
Others were rescued drifting on the reef.
It wasn't a tiff – many were found dead and stiff!
All the beaches did shrink – there was mayhem.

We were stuck on the mountain without food or water.

The God of mercy was nowhere to help us.
We prayed and prayed and prayed to no avail.
December 26, 2004 turned into untold grief.
Fortunately lady luck came our way.
We were finally whisked to safety – thank God.
I was left a nerve wreck with regular panic attacks.
I survived by a whisker – to tell the tale of the Tsunami.

**23 Free verse**

**Title: Murder in the Neighbourhood**

Today, something horrible has happened.
We're in grief as a community.
Taken away ruthlessly is one of us.
Sadly bludgeoned in cold-blood,
Butchered mercilessly for the sake of his colour,
Tell me, why? Oh no!
Did the stork choose to be white?
Oh, tell me.
Did the crow choose to be black?
Oh, tell me.
Did the leopard choose to have spots?
Oh, tell me.
Did he ever choose to be an Albino?

Something is amiss in this locality.
Today he lies dead without a heart.
Mercilessly ripped out for rituals,
Ritual murder pays not – oh hear!
We must engage our youths, they must fear evil.
To prosper in business needs no Albino blood.
Marketing and management makes business tick.
Oh hear, that's the proper ritual for success.
Food takeaways need no magic to sell hot dogs.
It's the worst evil to murder Albinos for rituals.
A business entity succeeds through hard work.
Fellas, let's not forget the law of Karma,
Self-serving evil actions will come back to worry us.

Even if no one had seen us commit the crime,
One of us is dead today.

Killed undercover of the starry night,
One day justice shall prevail.
He didn't deserve to die – oh hear!
Why spill blood for the sake of rituals?
Albinism is not a death sentence.
It doesn't make him a lesser being.
Why kill him in cold blood?.
Oh hear, did he deserve this brutal end?
No, no, not at all – I swear blind!
Our God forbid murder – judgement day is nigh!
The evil that humanity do – shall catch up with them!

**24 Free verse**

**Title: Free Spirit – It's Halloween!**

Fear not my spirit – you're now a free spirit.
Roam this world freely – you belong here!
The body you once occupied,
It's now dead and buried.
It succumbed to cancer of the lungs,
You left it and you're now an incarnate.


Fear not my spirit, float freely – you lives on.
That skeletal body you once dwelled in,
Is no longer part of you? It's all gone!
Gone to the undertaker, to be reduced to ashes,
It's all gone under the earth – into the moist grave.
Fear not my spirit – you're a survivor.


It's Halloween tonight.
Roam the city – spook them.
Its Halloween tonight scare them.
Show them you live on,
Show them you can have fun.
Show them you once walked the face of earth.


Scare them - turn on and off the lights.
Tidy the kitchen let them feel your presence.
Appear to your granddaughter as an apparition.
Tell her a folktale in her sleep.
Pack her school lunch.
Visit mum and dad in their sleep.


Its Halloween tonight, let them feel your presence.
Pinch your wife's bum in her sleep, tease her.

Its Halloween tonight – let her feel your presence.
Turn into a ball of fire at the beach tonight.
Show them you're above death.
Trick and spook, Treat and scare. It's Halloween!

Fear not my spirit – you're now a free spirit.
Turn up at your former local pub.
Haunt them for a laugh. On the dance floor – scare them!
Let them scatter like birds in fear – its Halloween tonight.
Fear not my spirit – you defeated death by embracing it.
You now belong to the after world – enjoy!

**25 Free verse**

**Title: Single and Ready to Mingle**

I loved my marriage and wanted it to work.
I was a good listener – I could not harm a fly.
I was a subservient wife – very religious!
The last straw that broke the camel's back was
When he cheated on me with my best friend,
I send him packing when I caught him snogging.
I walked out, I bowed out – we divorced!
I'm single and ready to mingle.
Who said broken hearts can't be mended?
I'm single and ready to mingle.
Life begins at forty – I've come of age.
I'm starting anew – age is just a number!
I'm young at heart – I'm raring to go.
After the storm there is always a fresh start.
After divorce there is always a new beginning.
Who said lonely hearts are supposed to be lonely forever?
I'm single and ready to mingle.
Who said dating sites are not for the elderly?
I'm single and ready to mingle.
Who said an old woman doesn't know 'selfie' and sexting?
I can skype – I can tweet, in search of love!
'WhatsApp' is for us all – Viber is now international!
Skype is ruling the world – it's my hope for a fresh start.
Facebook has gone viral – I'm single and ready to mingle!
Who said the 'adults' bedroom game' is no longer for me?
I'm single and ready to mingle.
Who said the dance floor is not for an old woman?
I'm single and ready to mingle.
Who said Strictly Come Dancing is not for me?
I'm bubbly and ready to dance.

I need to get my life back – I need to move on.
I need a date! I need a cuddle on Valentine's Day.
Woohoo! I'm single and ready to mingle!

**26 Free verse**

**Title: Part of Me Is Missing...**

Hats off! To you my adoptive parents!

For taking me as one of your own,

For the hugs, for the love,

You gave me all these years,

I can't thank you enough.

You're the cream of the crop.

You provided for me – you christened me!

You nursed me when I was poorly.

In my soiled pants you hugged me.

When I wetted the bed you didn't pick on me.

Every birthday of mine,

Every achievement to my sleeve,

You pampered me with presents and cuddles.

The more I appreciate the best upbringing you gave me.

The more I need to know my biological parents.

I don't mean to offend you,

My great adoptive parents,

I just need closure to this hurtful hole in my heart.

A penguin can never be a duck.

Blood is thicker than water.

Even though my biological parents were not there for me,

Part of me is missing – part of me is hurting.

I need to say hello to them!

I need to know whether they have tattoos!

I need to know whether I resemble them.

I need a cup of tea with them to ask them – why?

I want my kids to hug and tease them – to play with their cheeks.

I want my kids to go trick and treat with them on Halloween Night.

I want to go out and have fun with them on Bonfire Night.
Christmas comes but once a year – I need a meal with them.
Part of me is missing – part of me is hurting.

**27 Free verse**
**Title: Swansea on a Saturday Night**

All roads lead to Swansea on a Saturday night.
From Mumbles, from Morriston,
They all get to Swansea.
From Neath, from Cardiff – all roads lead to Swansea.
From London, From Scotland,
The motorway leads to Swansea.
People from all walks of life,
Dine and wine in the heart of Swansea,
They come to Swansea for a night out.
They come in droves for a drink in Swansea.
Without fear or racial prejudice they merry-make,
Swansea is colour blind when it comes to partying.
Swansea knows no race on a Saturday night out.
They're all party animals – they consume beer wildly.
With hardly a care – the all 'bum jive',
Boom – boom, Bo-o boom, goes the raucous music.
The youth, the middle aged and the senior citizens,
They raise their glasses to a toast all in smiles.
They have something in common,
They buy and drink the Brains Beer.
The beer of good cheer – the blend of Wales!
The White, the Asians and the Black,
They all mix on the dance floor.
They dance, they hug, and they kiss on the dance floor.
The swap phone numbers – they whisper in each other's ears.
They find love in Swansea on a Saturday night out.
Some drink till the witching hour.
Others dine and wine till the cows come home!
It's a hive of activities – revelers drink beer merrily.

They laugh and joke sweetly.
They play poker as a team.
Don't risk missing the funny – all roads lead to Swansea.
Come and join the funny!
Swansea on a Saturday night – thrills!

**28 Free verse**
**Title: Christmas Day in Swansea**

The streets are deserted – it's like a ghost town.
It looks like the scary Welsh Dragon has been let loose.
And people seem to be hiding for dear life.
The roads are quiet and empty.
The city centre is as quiet as death.
A few pigeons are flying around the city,
Seemingly, spreading the news,
Thank God it's Christmas!
Decorated Christmas trees in the heart of Swansea,
Are reminders that Swansea is in celebrating mood,
Streets lights are continuously flashing.
Red, amber, green is the sequence.
But, there is no traffic to regulate.
Depictions of Santa are hanging in the neighbouring houses.
The aromatic smell of roasting turkey,
 Keeps coming to my nostrils,
Softly – softly Christmas melodies fill the atmosphere.
People are indoors celebrating Christmas.
Kids are kin to open their Christmas presents on Boxing Day.
Hippity hip hooray – hippity hip hooray!
There is nothing better like Christmas Day in Swansea.

**29 Free verse**

**Title: Payday Lender**

I'm the prey – you're the predator.

I'm the hunted - you're the hunter.

I'm the victim – you're the victor.

It's a cat and mouse game.

You're the python.

You attract your prey by your gleaming colours.

Your tactics are second to none.

Your crocodile smile – your sweet talk,

Your crocodile tears – your baby face,

Deceived me into taking a loan,

You lured me into permanent debt.

Your crocodile smile - your sweet talk,

Made me believe the interest was affordable,

I know you're in business – you want profit.

But – it's not an even playing field.

Your interests are outrageous.

You want to make a kill in one go.

You want to get rich quick.

You made me pay double the amount.

I borrowed a fiver – I paid back a tenner.

She borrowed a tenner – she paid back twenty.

The moment I paid it back – you offered me another loan.

Is this being merciful or you're encouraging me into debt.

Are you not grooming me into a debt addict?

Stop making me a disciple of debt.

This get rich quick attitude must stop.

Your excessive interests must stop!

God have mercy on you – you feckless Payday Lender.

**30 Free verse**

**Title: Drug Addict**

Day in, day out, he is on the streets of Swansea.

From High Street to Wind Street,

From the train station to the Guildhall,

He roams the streets asking for spare change.

He seems to have mastered the art of begging.

He always says he is lacking ten pence for his bus fare home.

Those who don't know his tricks will give generously.

At the crack of dawn he roams the pavements of Night Clubs.

Searching for coins dropped by revelers the previous night,

He scavenges all the wheelie bins in the City Centre.

His aim is to find goodies for resale to feed his drugs habit.

He thinks puffing on hand – rolled cannabis joint is cool.

He assumes taking heroine makes him a demigod.

He worships cocaine – he thinks it makes him wiser.

Cider after cider is the order of the day.

A day without drugs makes him sick.

A day without drugs makes his head spin.

His eyes are permanently red - he has mood swings.

His hair is unkempt – he detests taking a bath.

He has no interest in finding a job – he has lost hope in life.

He sleeps rough in the cemetery.

He sleeps rough in the stinking sewer pipes.

He sleeps rough in the car park.

Depression is catching up with him.

He doesn't want to seek help from Support Workers.

Maybe he doesn't know that,
He can get help with his addiction.
Can society just watch him perish?
He needs a helping hand to fight his demons.
He is one of us – he deserves better.

**31 Free verse**

**Title: Good-bye Winter Floods**

Good- bye, good- bye, winter floods!

You're a devil in our midst.

You're a demon which needs exorcism.

Cheerio, cheerio to you – frost bites and snow!

Farewell to you winter floods.

You deserve to be thrown at the back of our minds.

In Wales, Scotland and England – you caused havoc.

You're a coward –you flooded our homes mercilessly.

You eroded our beautiful coastal areas unsparingly.

You ripped apart power- lines, railway- tracks and trees.

You brought railway transport to a halt.

The bees and the butterflies will curse you forever

For destroying their habitat,

Spring is in sight now –Daffodils are blooming.

That's the best revenge nature can offer.

Now, we can dance around in the sunny weather.

It's good riddance that you're gone winter floods!

Gone into the dust bin of memory lane,

Gone to be devoured by the gods of the spring sunshine,

It is spring time – summer is sure to come!

We can finally enjoy the glorious sunshine,

Whilst we repair your damages – coward winter floods!

Rest in peace- coward winter floods!

No-one will be missing – winter 2014!

## 32 Free verse
### Title: Halt This Football Madness

Hey fellas – hey football fans!
You're misfiring – you're over the top!
Stop these monkey chants.
You're dealing with black footballers, not monkeys.
Stop booing them – they're professionals.
To be born black does not make them monkeys.
Do they have tails? Do they have furs of monkeys?
Halt this football madness – it's inhuman!

They have God -given skills – they're talented footballers.
They play for Manchester United – they play for England!
They're proud to be British – they raise high the Union Jack!
They play for Swansea – they play for Cardiff!
Stop calling them –'Choc ice'- black man in a white man's heart!
They're not cannon fodder, they're not guinea pigs.
Halt this football madness – halt this football racism.

Football skills know any colour – money knows no colour!
It's a rainbow world - football fans!
Be accommodating - be tolerant.
Black footballers are here to stay – embrace them!
These monkey chants must go cold turkey!
What is good to goose is also good for gander.
Halt this football madness – halt this football racism!
Shun football racism – It's cancerous.

Stop these monkey chants – they trigger hatred.
Football racism belittles human advancement.
Sapp Blatter says no to football racism!
Why can't we dance to his tune in weeding out football racism?
Halt this football madness forthwith – let it die young!

**33 Free verse**

**Title: Benefits Cheat**

The voice of reason is echoing.
It's echoing on the Brecon Beacons Mountains!
The voice of conscience is reverberating.
It's reverberating on Pen y Fan Mountain,
The highest mountain in South Wales,
The voice is loud and clear.
Wake up and smell the coffee, scrounger!
The voice of conscience is here to warn you.
The gods of sanity are angry with you.
They're the custodians of good morals.
They are the keepers of heaven and earth.
You're an embarrassment to the nation.
You're milking the taxpayer.
You think it's cool to cheat.
You pretend to be disabled.
Yet, in reality you're as fit as a rugby player.
You're tarnishing the image of the disabled citizens.
You think you're invincible.
You think you're superior to me!
I'm immortal – I'm the voice of reason!
I'm the voice of conscience – I'm the custodian of sanity.
You pretend to be single when claiming benefits,
Yet, in reality you're living with a working partner.
You're milking the taxpayer.
You're reaping where you did not sow – you're a parasite.
You're feeding on the blood of hard working citizens.
You're committing a crime – you're dicing with
imprisonment.

Information about your cheating is now known.
Inform the authority before the net closes in.
The net is closing in – soon they'll catch you.
You'll be obliged to pay back the loot.
Failing which, you'll rot in jail.
'Own up' – yes take responsibility.
Crime does not pay – cheating makes you sink low.
Get a job, couch potato – get a life, benefits cheat!
Benefits are for the needy, not for the greedy!
Being a scrounger is self-denial – it's a ticking time bomb.
You're shooting yourself in the foot.
Do you hear me benefits cheat?
The voice of conscience is only warning you!
It's not if they catch you – it's when!

**34 Free verse**
**Title: Wonder with Me**

Drift with me – float with me.

Wonder with me!

Heaven, do you exist?

Are you a planet like Earth?

Do you have Welsh cakes?

Talk to me heaven! Can I locate you on a map?

Are you as beautiful as the Gower Peninsula?

Do you have buildings as tall as The Shard?

Do you have a place for poets?

I speak the Queen's English.

What's your official language heaven?

Do you speak in tongues?

Do they speak Aramaic?

Are you developed as yet?

Or you're another Somalia – lawless and destroyed!

Many great thinkers have left this world,

Are they of good use there?

Maybe they're now couch potatoes.

Drift with me – float with me.

Wonder with me!

We have continents here on earth,

If I die in Africa will I go to an African heaven?

If I die in America will I go to an American heaven?

Drift with me - float with me.

Wonder with me!

I heard that there're angels in heaven,

Are they paid like ministers here on Earth?

How are they chosen?

Are they selected in beauty contests?
Heaven! Do you exist?
Or – it's hearsay.
Drift with me – float with me.
Wonder with me!

**35 Free verse**

**Title: At the Beach after Dark**

She sits at the beach after dark.

The moonlit sky is awash with stars.

Gazing to the sea – she clasps her cheek.

In the other hand she clutches a posy of flowers.

Her mind is wrestling with wild thoughts.

There is no trace of a smile on her face.

She is here to reflect on her husband's death,

He died at sea, after the cruise boat capsized.

His body was never found.

She is here to appease his spirit.

She is here to put closure to his death.

She wants to inform him that,

 Her daughter has started school,

She wants to plead with sea gods,

To reveal his remains for burial,

She wants to plead with the sea gods to take care of him.

She wants to tell the late husband that,

 She misses him and loves him.

Instinctively- she senses the presence of a ghost.

Could it be him? Why do ghosts appear at night?

Whilst still marveling,

The silhouette of a merman smiles at her.

 She throws a posy of flowers into the sea, in tears.

In bewilderment she walks away murmuring,

He lives on; he lives on – my husband.

At the beach after dark,

**36 Free verse**
**Title: The Sea**
Seeing believes.
Come and see the sea.
Its azure still waters run deep.
As I gazes upon the sun-drenched tranquil sea,
Dazzling rays of sun glint.
Swiftly, violent waves spring.
They bounce back and forth quirkily.
Crashing forcefully on the soggy sand,
Swiveling ferociously on the damp sand,
As the waves retreat,
Debris is scooped into the sea.
Divulging the sea's harshness to my naked eye,
It is as fierce and ruthless as a black witch!
It makes me believe convincingly that,
Misfortunes are embedded in its waters.
The Titanic sinks to its seabed.
Migrants trying to reach Europe drown.
Soldiers fought at sea never returned home.
Scuba divers never saw the light of day.
Unmarked graves are strewn in this sea.
Could the sea be concealing mermaids and mermen?
Could the sea be a silent assassin?
I still wonder and continue to ask sadly.
Did the sea swallow the Malaysian plane flight MH370?

**37 Free verse**

**Title: Adulterous Cleric**

Ding-dong, ding- dong, goes the church bell.

In his lavish suit he enters the church.

The man we all respect, our church pastor.

The man who gives us salvation,

He prays for the sick and the bereaved.

He teaches us not to commit adultery.

But – there is a dark side to this servant of the lord.

He is hypocritical – our church pastor is lustful.

He is having an affair with the deacon's wife.

He is always at the beach after dark, smooching her.

He arranges sham prayer meetings – to romp with her.

The deacon's husband doesn't know a thing.

He doesn't smell a rat – he is full of praise for the pastor.

The deacon's wife gives in to the pastor's advances affably.

The pastor is so discreet in arranging the romping sittings.

Only God knows that his chosen servant is a rotten egg.

Walls have ears – parishioners are hearing!

Swansea has eyes – it's watching with an eagle's eye.

It's a matter of time before they're cornered.

Pastor! You're sitting on a powder keg.

Your voracious appetite for a married woman must stop.

Man of the cloth, control your libido, the net is closing in.

Spare the church from shame. Boo! It's disgusting.

**38 Free verse**
**Title: Traffic Jam**

It beggars belief that the dinner lady,
And the doctors are late for work again.
It's the third time in a row this week.
Children at school need their dinner.
Patients in hospital wards need their doctors.
Traffic is moving at a snail's pace.
It is as slow as an asthmatic snail.
Drivers are honking in frustration.
It's not their fault to be honest,
You're to blame traffic policeman.
It's your fault man in uniform.
You're stage managing this traffic jam.
You're delaying traffic to get kickbacks.
Motorists are having a raw deal.
You're exaggerating faults on vehicles.
Your aim is to solicit for bribes from motorists,
Making a kill by charging spot fines,
You're ripping them off their hard earned pound sterling.
Aren't you walking on hot coal cop?
Justice will spit in your face soon!
Stop ducking and diving,
Stop milking the Treasury.
'Greasing your palms' with dirty dosh,
Tarnishes your image as a trustworthy cop,
Parasitic cop! Stop sucking the blood of motorists.
Sergeant, stop this unholy traffic jam of intent.
Be the light of the nation – not a conning cop.
Be a law enforcer not a law breaker.

Be the salt of the earth not a swindler.
It's a matter of time before you're caught on camera.
They'll name and shame you – highway patrol cop!

**39 Free verse**

**Title: Leaping Into the Dark**

Hang on! Spare a minute.

Look me straight into the eye.

Listen to me, spoilt brat.

Be attentive! Cooperate!

Being the only child is not an excuse.

Don't lose foresight.

Bunking lessons is a leap into the dark.

You're opening 'floodgates' of illiteracy.

'Own up' to your fiascos.

Soon and very soon,

You'll be a disciple of illiteracy.

Soon or later, you'll be a daredevil criminal.

Sooner or later, you'll be a social misfit.

You're leaping into the dark, by taking drugs.

You're leaping into the dark by being a gangster.

Gang culture is suicidal – take a step back!

Before you've a brush with the law,

Take a step backwards!

Before you rot in jail,

Back off, back off and back off!

Before you leap into the darkest moist grave,

Before you become statistics at the cemetery,

Irresponsible behaviour is a leap into the dark.

**40 Free verse**

**Title: If I Could Turn Back the Clock**

How Daffodils bloom, how Daffodils wither,

Is an indicator of change as an essence of life?

How the sun sets, how the sun rises,

It's an indicator of how time changes.

If I could turn back the clock,

I would want to be young again.

And reclaim my childhood,

Which I lost to the chubby 'freebooter',

Who took away my innocence in my sleep?

He deflowered me without my consent.

It was disgusting.

If I could rewind the clock,

I would want his past to catch up with him.

I would want him to be arrested for his evil deeds.

If I could rewind the clock,

I would want to choose the husband of my choice.

Not this chubby one, who was imposed on me.

I'm trapped, trapped and trapped in a hell-hole marriage!

This loveless, lifeless arranged marriage is a pain.

It's a matter of time before I do a runner!

I swear blind, if I could turn back the clock – for sure,

No way, would I ever marry – this opportunist.

**41 Free verse**

**Title: Sanctity of Life**

To live life, is to love life.

To love life, is to live life.

Life is for living – it is sacred.

Life's prized – It must be preserved.

It's a right to all humanity.

He is happy to breathe life – she is too!

They're happy go lucky beings.

They're not in a hurry to die!

What makes him want to cut their lives short?

What makes her want to spill innocent blood?

What makes them kill women and children?

Beheading humans in cold- blood,

Is barbaric and evil in equal measure,

It impugns human saneness.

It is as bizarre as it is perverse.

Is it for rituals? Is it for a cause?

Or, they're just trigger happy ogres.

Murderers – heartless murderers!

The 'how, when, why and where' of our deaths,

Can only be decided by our maker,

Those who live by the sword,

Indeed – die by the sword!

To love life, is to preserve life.

**42 Free verse**

**Title: Money Can't Buy Hygiene**

He is well to do – her landlord!

He owns houses in Swansea.

He lives in a quiet cul-de-sac.

He doesn't give a damn to cleanliness.

The cleanliness is near to godliness dictum

Is not part of his vocabulary nor is it in his blood.

The moment she entered his house,

She was met by an assorted stench.

A home-grown smell to kill pong sealed the air.

Rotting garbage was all over the place.

Rats were having a party with hardly a care.

One step into his bedroom – she was shell-shocked!

Clothes tossed on the bed were an eyesore.

Dirty pants near a pizza takeaway were smelly.

They made her want to throw up.

Fag ash on the floor was sickening.

It was a remainder of his chain-smoking.

Empty cans of cider strewn all over the room

were cues of his binge drinking.

Cob webs made a rail track like pattern on the ceiling.

Dog poo in a heap near the living room door was

nauseating!

It quickly sent a shiver down her spine.

She plucked the courage to persuade him to tide his house.

He tore her apart by saying: Don't you know that,

Despite the stench a chicken's coop is the

golden palace of the cockerel.

What you see is what you get –I don't harm a fly.

Do you think I'm a stickler for cleanliness?
Money comes first and it matters to me.
Have you brought your rent?
Pay! Your rent is late! – don't overstay your welcome!

**43 Free verse**

**Title: Hear Me Cry**

Look me in the eye – what you see is reality,

I'm a woman of colour – Colette is my name.

It's neither an African nor an Asian name.

It's a cool British name of French origin.

It means victory, I'm a winner.

Swansea is where I belong.

No-one can take that from me.

I belong to Wales – I'm British.

I'm a citizen not a stranger!

I'm after you wishers of doom!

I'm after you 'sickos'.

I'm pouncing at you with vengeance!

Why do you discriminate me at night?

Why do you deny me a taxi at night?

Alas! Your discrimination makes me sick.

Being black does not make me a prostitute.

To be born black is not a curse.

All humanity's blood is red.

Did the crow choose to be black?

Did the stork choose to be white?

Did the leopard choose to have spots?

Don't judge the book by its cover.

Being black doesn't make me a lesser being.

I've a razor sharp brain – I'm not a slag!

I'm neither a prostitute nor a scrounger.

I'm an earnest worker – I'm a striver not a shirker.

I'm a workaholic – not a 'pay- as -you –go' slut.

I'm not after, 'pay-as-you- go' sex after dark!

Give me a lift –I just need a taxi home!
It's not for free, I pay.
Money knows no colour!

**44 Free verse**

**Title: St Jude – Mother of All Storms**

As we turned our clocks one hour backwards
To signal the onset of the British winter time,
The Met Office issued an amber alert warning.
Mother Nature was about to turn her back on us.
She was about to spit venom on the United Kingdom.
A fierce storm, St Jude, was brewing in the Atlantic.
As the dark clouds swirled over Southern Britain,
We all went numb – hysterically we waited for Jude.
The inevitable was nigh – St Jude was coming forcefully.
In no time heavy rain pounded the coastal areas.
It never rains but it pours – gusty winds battered the UK.
From Cardiff to London – blustery winds caused mayhem.
Flying debris unleashed terror on motorists.
Torrential rain wreaked havoc – trees fell on cars and buildings.
Homes were left without power – buildings collapsed.
It's so sad some didn't make it in this mother of all storms.
As the sun shines again after the storm – questions still remain.
Did the emergency services do a good job?
Could they have done it differently?
Isn't it time to cut all the tall trees near our buildings?
Prevention is better than cure its better safe than sorry.
To all those affected by the storm St Jude – hope is not lost.
Jesus Christ made this promise – Matthew28:20,
'…and surely I am with you always, to the very end of the age.'

**45 Free verse**

**Title: Roaring Lioness**

The lioness is not scared of the dark.

It roars with exuberance in pitch black night.

Its eyes glow in a moonless night sky,

Ready to pounce on its prey,

Its loud roar affirms openly

That it is the queen of the jungle.

It takes no chances when it comes to finding its supper.

It will pounce on its prey till the bitter end.

Its last breath is punctuated with a roar of courage.

It'll fight to its last drop of blood.

It'll die protecting its cubs – it'll die fending for its brood.

It doesn't give up – it rises to the occasion.

Joana Lumley is a lioness – she rises to the occasion.

She is a lady of grit – she is a heroine.

She is unbreakable – she is a warrior.

She knows no surrender – she knows no retreat.

She fought a good and just fight.

She fought for the Gurkhas' rights to live in Britain.

She fought for the voiceless.

She is the one - she is a powerful woman.

Go Lumley! Go girl! – You're a roaring lioness!

Girl power rules the world!

The kitchen is no longer the rightful place of a woman.

Indeed -women are meant to reach the stars.

You're the queen of justice – go girl, the world needs you.

You're the pride of Britain – you're the pride of the Gurkhas!

You fought for the good of humanity.

You fought for the Gurkhas' rights to be British.
Go girl! Go Joanna – roar on, roar lioness!
You're the cream of the crop!

**46 Free verse**

**Title: Reclusive Friend**

Hear me cry – reclusive friend!
Why are you detached from reality?
We're next door friends for real.
Neither of us is superior to the other.
We're as equal as flies on a heap of poo!
A smile a day makes us live longer.
If I smile at you – smile in turn!
If I wave a hand at you do likewise.
A good turn deserves another.
Why are you as proud as a peacock?
You're so unpredictable like a volcano or a Tsunami?
You are neither a volcano nor a Tsunami.
You're my friend – a human being with conscience.
Is this what you call friendship?
To ignore when your friend says – Happy New Year!
Is this what you call being classy?
To ignore the funeral of my grandson,
Is this what you call pride?
To bin the present I give you on your birthday,
Your seclusion scares me.
Swallow your pride, pal.
Friends are meant to be there for each other.
I was taught to love thy friend!
Why not do the same?
Make friends before you need them.

**47 Free verse**

**Title: The Stick Fighter from Qunu**

From the rolling hills and valleys of Qunu, it all started.

Stick- fighting groomed you into a brave warrior.

Stick- fighting taught you resilience and endurance!

It taught you team play and collective thinking.

It taught you reconciliation with your rivals.

From the sun-kissed roads of Qunu.

Mandela the stick-fighter – your long walk to freedom began!

From a mere herd boy you transcended into a freedom fighter.

From the cell of Robben Island – You came out a unifier!

Mandela the stick fighter – you fought racism head on!

You extended an olive branch to your jailers.

You had a dream for a better South Africa!

You had a dream – a vision for a better world!

We shout and shout and shout praise,

To you, Madala Nelson Rohlihlahla Mandela,

We cry and cry and cry,

Buckets loads of tears for you, Madiba,

From Cape to Cairo – Australia to the Americas,

You touched all – Mandela! You came, you conquered!

You gave peace a chance.

You came for the greater good of humanity!

Now that you have joined the world of immortals,

Continue to watch over the rainbow nation,

Visit the corrupt leaders of the ANC in their sleep.

And remind them of what you lived for.

Unbreakable reconciliation and economic freedom for all,

You walked the talk – you're a winner!
Rest in peace – Mandela the stick- fighter from Qunu.

**48 Free verse**

**Title: Family Squabble**

Come rain, come thunder – come hell, come fire.

Through thick and thin – you'll remain my brother.

Misunderstandings cannot put us asunder.

Blood is thicker than water.

We shared the same breast milk.

We share the same duvet as we grew up.

Yes, we have reached crossroads.

Yes, we have argued loads over money.

Yes, we have teased each other.

But, we have something in common.

We cannot wipe our birth mark.

Same mother, same father makes our connection tighter.

Reconsider your standpoint brother – I still need you.

Two wrongs cannot make a right.

Come to your senses.

Brother against brother defies logic.

War of words doesn't pay.

We can't fight over our dead father's will.

His riches belong to him.

Come on dude – come on brother.

A dead man's fortune, can't strain our relationship.

Forget about inheritance money.

I miss your smile, brother.

Our dead father's wealth can't make us enemies.

Let's be men enough and toil for our own wealth.

Let's be men enough to reconcile.

It's time to bury the hatchet.

Bog off, inheritance money.

Let it be donated to cats and dogs charities.

It's time to be a family again.

Brother, brother, together as one!
United we stand, divided we fall.
Two hands are better than one.

**49 Free verse**

**Title: I've Got My Eyes To Thank.**

I see eye to eye with my eyes.

I agree with them in total.

The basis of my decisions stems from what I see.

I believe more in what I see than hear.

I've got my eyes to thank,

For spotting the beauty in my wife.

We got married, because I was beauty conscious.

Seeing believes – Indeed it's true.

I witnessed the opening of the 2012 Olympic Games.

There are still naked people living in the Amazon Rain Forest.

I've got my eyes to thank for discovering that.

Where you there at the Queen's Diamond Jubilee celebrations?

I've got my eyes to thank for seeing it live.

Did you see Mohammed Farah win gold at the Olympic Games?

Woohoo! My eyes did a good job that day.

Everything unfolded in my full view – I was over the moon.

A blind man cannot lead a blind man.

I've got my eyes to thank for leading me to the Pizza shop.

Have you been to Mars?

I've got my eyes to thank.

I saw Curiosity Rover landing on Mars.

The power of vision in my eyes is God given.

My eyes are my guardian angel,

I shall not want.

**50 Free verse**

**Title: I can hear**

Even though I'm not at the battle front,

My ears are alert – I can hear.

I can hear continuous gunfire,

In Aleppo and Homs,

I can hear the wailing of children.

Shouting for help in vain,

The elderly trapped and trapped,

In dilapidated buildings, are gasping for air.

I can hear the desperate crying,

Of new born babies, frantically crying for milk,

Near the dead bodies of their mothers,

I can hear the voices of the Syrian refugees.

In Lebanon, Jordan and Turkey,

They're speaking loud and clear.

We want food, tents and clean water – not war.

I can hear the UN speaking authoritatively,

Assad, Assad! No to chemical weapons on civilians!

I can hear the gassed civilians – dying in agony.

I plead, hey, the caring world,

Wake up and smell the coffee!

Come to the rescue of innocent civilians.

Even though I try hard not to listen,

I continue to hear, the last breath of a dying child,

I can hear a child crying in the wilderness,

The voice is coming closer and closer.

It's loud and clear. We want peace not war.

We want food and medicine.

I can hear what the child wants,

But, I'm powerless and penniless as a church mouse,

I can hear the fading voice of a child pleading,

Bashar al – Assad, we want to live.
The voice of the Syrian child echoes in the mountains.
We are being gassed here – where is thy neighbour?

**51 Free verse**

**Title: The Taste of the Pudding ...**

You can't say grapes are sour, before you taste them,

I've tasted grapes – indeed they're sour.

I've tasted honey – indeed it is sweet.

I've tasted French fries – indeed they're cool!

I've tasted Tikka Masala – indeed it is fabulous.

The taste of the pudding is in the eating!

You can't say Oats porridge is cool, before you taste it.

I've been there – I tasted it.

My taste buds can declare that sugar is sweeter than salt!

I've been there – I tasted them all.

I love hot spices because I've tasted them.

The taste of the pudding is in the eating.

I trust my sense of taste, when I say,

Grapes are sour, sugar is sweeter than salt.

Honey is sweeter than water, I've been there.

I sampled them all.

The taste of the pudding is in the eating.

**52 Free verse**

**Title: Love Letter from the War Front**

Hi, honey.

Hope you're keeping well.

I'm here at the war front.

I'm trying to look positive for the future.

I've your photo as a reminder of our love.

I carry it every day together with my gun.

Even though, I'm far afield,

Your photo helps me to connect with you.

I can touch, feel and kiss it when I think of you.

I can feel your presence and beauty on this photo.

On my dull days your beautiful photo,

Can put a smile on my face,

I always sleep holding your photo close to my chest.

If I touch, feel and kiss your photo,

It helps me to reconnect with you.

Touching and feeling your photo is therapeutic.

It helps me cope with your absence.

As you may know, absence makes the heart grow fonder.

You know it's difficult here at the war front,

With your photo close to my chest,

I know you'll be closer to my heart.

On your birthday I shall touch and feel the photo.

If peace permits I'll pop the champagne for it.

You know honey, touching believes.

If I touch and feel your photo,

It makes me have deep feelings for you.

I'll keep, feel and touch this photo daily,

As long as I'm still here at the war front.
It's a true reminder of our true love.
Wait for me honey.
I'll be home for Christmas, love you loads.
The call of duty is ending soon.
I'm coming home, to feel and touch you for real.
Kiss, kiss and kiss.

**53 Free verse**

**Title: Dead without a Trace**

He just disappeared into the woods,

And there was no trace of him.

Days pass without him coming home.

Family members were hopeful,

That he would be found sound and well,

They were highly hopeful,

That he would soon walk through the door,

Vigils one after the other were held for him.

Prayers were held for his safe return.

But Johnny remained unaccounted for.

Weeks went by without a trace of him.

Searches for him were intensified.

Ground and air search teams were deployed.

No-one came forward with a shred of information.

His kith and kin never gave hope.

As patience was running thin,

A dog walker became suspicious,

When her nostrils caught a bad smell,

The strong smell kept on coming.

There was a nearby bush.

She let go her dog – wigging its tail.

It was up for the search with speed.

She followed the dog anxiously.

Suddenly the dog came to a halt,

There it was a decomposing body.

In awe the dog walker alerted the cops.

After some forensic t test were done.

Dead without a trace – at last he was found.

Thanks to the dog walker.
 And the dog's good sense of smell,
He was finally laid to rest.

**54 Free verse**

**Title: The Great Escape**

He was dragged into a dark dungeon.
They blindfolded him – kidnappers.
And shoved him onto a wooden bench,
He couldn't see where he was.
His immediate environment was pitch-black.
He couldn't see his way out.
He started using his other senses.
To plan his way out,
Being blindfolded is not inability.
He thought as he refined his strategies.
He staggered to the door.
Using his hands to clear the way,
His listening skills were at work.
 Listening for footsteps of anyone near,
His sense of smell didn't pick anyone smoking.
It gave him the assurances that,
The chain smoking kidnapers had left.
When the blindfolded him,
They were smoking like a chimney.
He gave himself the urge.
The urge to get out from the dungeon quick,
Instinct played in his favour.
He used his hands to clear the way.
He struggled all the way out of the dungeon.
The moment he conquered,
 The last hurdle out of the dungeon,
He ripped off the cloth used to blindfold him.
And shouted, free at last nothing can conquer hope!

**55 Free verse**
**Title: Dawn of a New Era**
2011year of the people's power.
The land of the Pharaohs was in turmoil,
The Egyptian Revolution spread like veld fire.
At Tahrir Square they spoke with one voice.
Mubarak out! We want change. Back off, Mubarak!
No to a police state, no to a military state,
Yes to democracy – they chant!
On the eve of Hosni Mubarak's demise,
They sang and danced in wild abandon at Tahrir Square.
They hugged and kissed each other in contentment.
They barbecued lamb and ate hot meals in bliss.
They popped sparkling wine jubilantly.
They shared Egyptian sweets in camaraderie.
Elections came in no time,
And Morsi was proclaimed the winner.
Democracy was welcomed in all smiles.
One year later, the military was at it again.
Democracy was thwarted – it died a natural death.
Morsi was stripped from power in a bloodless knockout.
House arrest reduced him to a toothless bull dog.
A political dying horse - a shrinking violet,
The military plane took to the skies of Cairo,
To enforce a curfew and to spot hooligans,
To pacify Morsi's supporters,
And to subdue the voice of reason,
Could it be that Egypt is descending into a civil war?
Would there be sanity in Egypt?
Could the military be doves – birds of peace?

Or they're wolves in sheep's coats?
Could the elders be right?
In saying politics is a dirty game?
Shall they sing and dance again at Tahrir Square?
Shall there be dawn of a new era in Egypt?
Only God knows.

**56 Free verse**

**Title: Don't You Dare…**

They say when you're in Rome, do as the Romans do.
Even though they say so, this is not going to work for her,
She has her morals and beliefs –She has her food preferences.
She has no appetite for dog meat.
She doesn't feel like eating it, it's no go area for her.
You can take a horse to the river,
But, you can't force it to drink.
How dare you want to serve her dog meat?
Yes, some enjoy dog meat – it's their choice to do so.
Don't assume that what's sauce for goose is sauce for the gander.
She is a unique individual, In need of consumer protection.
Dog biltong is not a delicacy to her.
It's not her cup of tea – it's unpalatable.
Don't you dare serve dog meat to her again?
She has no voracious appetite for dog liver.
She values a dog as mankind's best friend.
How dare you want her to eat dog mincemeat?
She doesn't feel like eating dog meat,
A dog is like a baby to her.
It's against her integrity, it's against her ethics.
No, no and no – I swear blind.
In this cafeteria, in this restaurant,
Don't you dare serve her dog meat again?

**57 Free verse**
**Title: Guess What!**

My heart bleeds when I think of you – Zambezi land.
The land where my umbilical cord is entombed,
You're too cute to be abused.
You're too treasurable to be wasted.
You don't deserve to be taken for a ride.
They're looting in full view of kids – the politicians!
They're plundering your resources heartlessly.
Your elephants are being poisoned cold-bloodedly.
They want quick dosh from ivory.
You've bread and butter for all your inhabitants.
But, the butter is spread by the few.
The gold and the diamonds are for the mighty ones.
Your breasts have milk for all your offspring.
Only the broad-chested ones suck it all!
Survival of the fittest is worrisome.
The get rich quick attitude boggles the mind.
They get the lion's share – they enjoy your spoils.
Whilst the have-nots feed on crumbs,
Dog eat dog made me a broken man.
Years of destitution have left me demented.
Years of scavenging have left me frail.
If I don't see you morrow – keep the hope!
Keep going, remember I love you – I really do!
My remains shall be interred in your womb.
And my spirit shall roam the parliament building.
Haunting them- the looters, the big fish of nepotism!
Haunting them the bigwigs of corruption!

They're male, stale and pale!
Guess what! Their end is nigh.

**58 Free verse**
**Title; You Gave Me Wings To Fly**
Write on, write on!
Time is a wine press.
Those were your words – Mum.
Words of encouraging me as a budding poet,
You cajoled me to learn the nuts and bolts of the trade,
Mum, my tutor, my mentor – my heroine!
You gave me wings to fly.


I can't thank you enough – Mum.
For nurturing me in the ways of the lord,
You raised me up well.
You're the salt of the earth.
 And my earthly goddess,
You gave me wings to fly.


You taught me about clichés.
Clichés to use and those not to use,
You taught me about writing a clean poem.
A poem which is punchy and without grammatical lapses,
Your poetic language gave me a springboard and I nailed it.
You gave me wings to fly – to fly high unaided.


You reinvigorated me – you encouraged me!
To be a critical thinker, a sharpened sword,
Do you still remember what you said?
The more your poems are nearer home,
The better they're likely to be.
It made me smile and I gave it a try.
Here I am - a bolstered poet!

Mum, mama – mother of all mothers!
Mother of courage – mother with heart made of steel!
I can't thank you enough – for inspiring me.
You're second to none – you're the cream of the crop!
Sweet mother – my heroine, my mentor,
You gave me wings to fly.

Your oratory skills, your eagle's eye,
Made me a meticulous poet and a keen editor,
Now that you're old and frail,
It's now my turn to mentor you.
It's now my turn to protect and guide you.
It's now my turn to give you wings to fly.

Mother of all mothers – sweet mother,
High five – you groomed another poet.
Walk tall with pride! You're the cream of the crop.
You gave me wings to fly – to reach the stars!
To write on and write on!

## 59 Free verse
### Title: Human kindness

To be human is to be kind.
To be kind is to be human.
Nothing can surpass human kindness.
Nothing can outshine human generosity.
People opened their hearts for them.
When they cried for help – the people of Nepal,
The earthquake left them homeless.
Shell-shocked and in dire straits,
They were left with nothing to survive on.
Human kindness came to their rescue.
Human kindness rallied behind them.
And people dug deep into their pockets,
And they gave them a token,
They donated in cash and kind.
They gave them hope and a fresh start.
They breathed life into their fading lives.
Sons and daughters of mother earth,
Showcased what it means to be human,
To be there for each other, through thick and thin,
No words can thank them enough,
They're the lions and lionesses of our time.
Forever and ever they remain God's shining stars!
Blessed are those hands that gave munificently.
May our maker bring forth countless blessings?
To the golden hands that give generously,
To be human is to be kind.
To be kind is to be human.
Nothing surpasses human kindness.
Our world will be poorer without exemplary givers.

## 60 Elegy
### Title: Leaf taken

Each day brings fresh thoughts of this leaf.
It was so green, it was so promising.
It was whispering with life.
It was tender and as fit as a steel nail.
It was flowering, blossoming and blooming.
When it was tragically taken away.
It's painful to talk about this leaf.
For the chlorophyll is no more.
It will always be a fatal blow to my conscience.
One leaf taken, it is you my friend, Charles.
Tears may dry but the loss lives on like footprints in the sand.
The pain you left in me flows like a river.
You were as harmless as a queen bee.
And as adorable as a rainbow,
You were my pillar of strength.
And a unifier in your family,
Now that the shepherd has been struck,
For sure the sheep will scatter.
My life shall never be the same.
I'm now a lone needle in the desert.
God gives, God takes, but why?
One leaf taken, it is you my friend.
Your death to me is a river of pain.
Drift and drift to eternity like a balloon.
Rest, rest and rest in peace great friend.
Till we laugh out loud again in eternity.

## 61 Monologue
## Title: Only dreaming

Snoring, duvet over my head.

Engulfed in a deep sleep.

Journeying in the past and the future.

Only my mind was at work,

Only my mind knew where I was,

I was enjoying this dream, on a snowy night.

It was vivid and real in my mind.

I was actually living the dream in my mind.

It was real, true and enjoyable.

The dream gave me hope.

Dreaming hugging angels made me a supernatural being.

Dreaming dining with angels gave me happiness.

Speaking in tongues with angels was stunning.

Dreaming flying in wonderland in a crimson rocket was soothing.

Dreaming being a millionaire gave me hope, comfort and satisfaction.

Dreaming in God's palace, gave me pride.

The king Midas' touch of gold blessed the dream.

Everything I touched, turned gold.

The plate I touched turned into gold.

The bed I slept on was pure gold.

As I suddenly woke up, my happiness ended abruptly.

When reality struck, I realized I was only dreaming.

Oh for heaven's sake!

I was still the usual Tom, sleeping in my shabby tiny room.

I was still the usual Tom, who could hardly afford a

meal.

I was still the city beggar, with torn clothes and hardly an underwear.

Fully awake and overwhelmed with disappointment, I shouted,

I was only dreaming, it is not real and it shall never be.

## 62 Monologue
### Title: I misfired

Every tick of a second signifies my end.

Day in day out,

My hours are numbered.

Every birthday signifies the maturity of the end.

My worst fear is inevitable.

It is looming like a storm.

They celebrated my birthday,

Mourning my death is inevitable.

My worst fear is looming.

It is on the horizon.

It is about to be real.

It drives me crazy to think of it.

It pricks my heart to know it for real,

That I am about to die,

The die has been cast.

It is too late to cry over spilt milk.

In a matter of days I will be dead.

I was a binge drinker.

Cider, one after the other was my breakfast.

Vodka after vodka was my lunch.

Champagne, one after the other graced my nights out.

Lambrini after Lambrini was my sleeping tablets.

Cocktail, one after the other was my pain killer.

Barcadi and coke nonstop,

Gave me Dutch courage at hen parties.

I was a contender in drinking contests.

It is too late for me to reform.

My liver is gone.

My worst fear is certain-to die of alcoholism.

If one can change, change now.

If one can learn, learn from my mistake.

Binge drinking is a killer, I misfired.

Don't dare do likewise?

My dark moments are obvious.

My fate is clear cut.

My voracious appetite for booze,

Has sentenced me to the moist grave,

Send me off, to eternity,

Whilst you sing and dance to the beat of the drum,

Farewell citizens, I misfired.

Binge drinking is a killer.

Beyond my grave, may you always remember

Binge drinking is a killer, I misfired.

Beyond my grave, may you always drink responsibly?

Farewell citizens, mine was a mistake to drink like a fish.

Masimba Mukichi